Cryptocurrency

Understanding Blockchain, Bitcoin Investing, Mining and Trading Digital Currencies

Arda Gauthier

© Copyright 2017 by Arda Gauthier - All rights reserved.

The following book is reproduced below with the goal of providing information that is as accurate and reliable as possible. Regardless, purchasing this book can be seen as consent to the fact that both the publisher and the author of this book are in no way experts on the topics discussed within and that any recommendations or suggestions that are made herein are for entertainment purposes only. Professionals should be consulted as needed prior to undertaking any of the action endorsed herein.

This declaration is deemed fair and valid by both the American Bar Association and the Committee of Publishers Association and is legally binding throughout the United States.

Furthermore, the transmission, duplication or reproduction of any of the following work including specific information will be considered an illegal act irrespective of if it is done electronically or in print. This extends to creating a secondary or tertiary copy of the work or a recorded copy and is only allowed with an express written consent of the Publisher. All additional rights are reserved.

The information in the following pages is broadly considered to be a truthful and accurate account of facts, and as such any inattention, use or misuse of the information in question by the reader will render any resulting actions solely under their purview. There are no scenarios in which the publisher or the original author of this work can be in any fashion deemed liable for any hardship or damages that may befall them after undertaking information described herein.

Additionally, the information in the following pages is intended only for informational purposes and should thus be thought of as universal. As befitting its nature, it is presented without assurance regarding its prolonged validity or interim quality. Trademarks that are mentioned are done without written consent and can in no way be considered an endorsement from the trademark holder.

Table of Contents

Introduction 1

Chapter 1: Basics of Bitcoin 3

Chapter 2: Best Sites to Buy Bitcoins 18

Chapter 3: Where to Store your Bitcoins 28

Chapter 4: Mining Bitcoin at Home 39

Chapter 5: Investing in Bitcoin 51

Chapter 6: What Is ICO? 63

Conclusion 73

Introduction

Congratulations on purchasing this book and thank you for doing so.

The following chapters will discuss everything you need to learn about Bitcoin and other cryptocurrencies. When you read this book, you will learn more about important topics such as Blockchain, Bitcoin, and other cryptocurrencies as well as how to trade in digital currencies and how to invest in Bitcoin.

Over the last 3 or 4 years, there has been tremendous interest in cryptocurrencies, especially Bitcoin. This is due to its phenomenal growth in recent years, its immense potential as well as its global reach. Think about an investor who bought $100 worth of Bitcoins in 2010. That investment is worth about $400,000 today. This goes to show just how impressive Bitcoin is.

If you want to share in the profits generated by Bitcoin, then you need to read this book to the end to understand the principles that govern cryptocurrencies. By doing so, you will learn all about the blockchain and how to mine Bitcoin. We trust that by the time you get to the end of the book, you will have learned enough about Bitcoin to consider investing in cryptocurrencies.

Now take a closer look at Bitcoin and find out where you fit best. Do you enjoy confirming transactions and generating new money? Then you should consider Bitcoin mining. Do you love sitting back and watching as your money grows? Then you probably should invest your money in Bitcoin. There are different ways of investing in Bitcoin so find one that is most suitable to you.

Whatever decision you make, we trust that it will benefit you immensely. Remember to thank us before the year 2017 is over because of the immense knowledge, wisdom and investment opportunities presented in this book.

There are plenty of books on this subject on the market, thanks again for choosing this one! Every effort was made to ensure it is full of as much useful information as possible. Please enjoy!

Chapter 1:

Basics of Bitcoin

What is Bitcoin?

Bitcoin is the first virtual, decentralized, digital currency. It is the most popular cryptocurrency in world today. Cryptocurrencies are digital currencies that use cryptography technology. Bitcoin is abbreviated BTC.

The Bitcoin payment system was designed by Satoshi Nakamoto, a pseudonym for a group of individuals, suspected to be American software engineers. The software designed to manage and administer Bitcoin was released in 2009.

Since then, improvements and updates have been made to the software by a group of developers who are mostly funded by the Bitcoin Foundation.

Is Bitcoin real, tangible money?

Bitcoin does not exist in any physical form. There are no Bitcoin notes or coins. Bitcoin exists as a string of characters with balances kept on a public ledger within the Bitcoin cloud network. All Bitcoin transactions are verified and recorded in a ledger known as the Blockchain.

Bitcoin is not controlled, issued or overseen by any government body. There is no central bank or other authority that manages or supervises Bitcoin.

Details of Bitcoin transactions

There are several genuine Bitcoin exchanges where you can buy Bitcoins. You can use fiat currencies like the pound, dollar or the Euro. Every time you purchase Bitcoins, you receive a set of keys. Each key consists of a long string of characters which are linked using an encryption algorithm.

You can compare Bitcoin public key to a bank account number. Your public key can be shared with any person especially when transacting. However, you should never share your private key with anyone. Bitcoin private key should be safeguarded as it compares to an ATM pin number.

You should only use your private key to authorize Bitcoin transactions. Your Bitcoins are kept securely in your digital wallet on your computer or mobile device.

Sending Bitcoins

Sending Bitcoins is as simple as sending an email. You can also purchase almost anything you want using Bitcoins. Professional programmers, known as miners, secure the Bitcoin network. Bitcoin miners are rewarded with newly minted Bitcoins for verifying transactions. Once transactions are confirmed, they are recorded on a transparent public ledger.

How does Bitcoin impact the world?

Bitcoin opens up an entirely new platform for innovations. The software used is 100% open source so anyone can review the code. Bitcoin is changing global finance precisely the same way the web changed publishing. When everyone has access to global markets, then great ideas will flourish.

Enables movement of money across borders

Using Bitcoin, traders and investors can move money from one country to another. Take the example of business owners in China. The government there limits the amount of money that can be transferred overseas. To overcome this challenge, residents buy substantial amounts of Bitcoin and then travel abroad and convert their Bitcoins back into hard currencies.

Bitcoin offers opportunities for businesses

- Bitcoins enables businesses to minimize their transactions fees.
- It does not cost anything to set up a Bitcoin account
- There are no chargebacks

- The bitcoin economy will bring in additional business

Increased investment in Bitcoin

Bitcoin has caught the attention of investors and traders from around the world. Bitcoin's attractiveness is based on its phenomenal growth and immense opportunities.

Institutions and individual investors who invested in Bitcoins in the past one year have received lucrative returns. In March 2016, 1 BTC was equivalent to $343. By January 2017, this amount had shot up to $1000, and by July it was at $4000. This represents more than tenfold increase in value. You, too, can invest in Bitcoin and benefit from this phenomenal growth.

Advantages of bitcoins over other currencies

- Bitcoins are transferred directly from person to person without going through a clearinghouse, so fees are much lower
- You can use Bitcoins in any country
- Your Bitcoin account cannot be frozen

- There are no pre-requisites or arbitrary limits set on Bitcoin users

Growth of Bitcoin over the years

2016: This year was significant for Bitcoin. Worth $425 at the start of the year, its value rose to $950 by year's end, representing a growth of more than 100%.

2014: The price of Bitcoin fell in 2014 with the highest value being $1000 which was recorded in January while the lowest price of $340 was observed in April. Bitcoin ended 2014 valued at $475, a fall of more than 100%.

2012: In December of 2011, the value of 1 BTC was $2, but a year later, the price as of December 2012 had jumped to $13 showcasing an increase of more than 700% in just one year.

The Blockchain

The blockchain is a public ledger of all Bitcoin transactions. It is a decentralized, cloud-based accounting system where all Bitcoin transactions such as transfer, purchase and sale of Bitcoins are recorded.

The blockchain is the backbone of Bitcoin. Other cryptocurrencies have adopted this technology as well. Its size keeps getting bigger as more and more blocks are added to it. New blocks are generated by Bitcoin miners within the network. Upon release into the system, the new blocks are recorded then added in chronological order.

This way, members of the blockchain can track all the transactions within the network. Being able to track a process is an excellent way of ensuring credibility of a system, especially one without central control. Members of the network are connected through a node. This makes it possible to access the Blockchain to check and confirm transactions.

Blockchain technology

Blockchain was initially developed to be the accounting system for managing all Bitcoin operations. It uses a technology known as DLT or Distributed Ledger Technology. DLT is primarily used for the verification of Bitcoin transactions.

Many other applications are beginning to adopt the blockchain ledger system. Blockchain can be configured to accommodate different kinds of transactions. It is proving especially prevalent in the financial sector. Trades completed at the markets can be registered on the blockchain so that everyone involved gets notified. This helps eliminate fraud and theft.

Software programmers can write code for other applications on the Blockchain. For instance, banks and other financial institutions are keenly observing blockchain with the hope of incorporating the system into the finance world. By using this method, there will always be a permanent record of transactions that cannot be deleted. Indelible records such as these are recommended for use in the accounting, business and finance sectors.

Adding blocks to the blockchain

The blockchain consists of individual blocks which are continually added to the system. Information pertaining to transactions is contained in an individual block. As soon as a single transaction is completed and added to the block, the block then joins the blockchain and becomes an integral part of the system. Blocks are therefore indelible, permanent records that are crucial to the blockchain.

Each block in the blockchain contains a hash of the previous transaction so that there is continuity when following up transactions. Blockchain design is such that transactions, once entered, cannot be deleted. Therefore, any transaction that takes place is recorded and has a permanent record.

Challenges of the Blockchain

In recent years, there has been growing concern about the rapidly growing blockchain. Every time a block is added to the blockchain, it increases the size and complexity of the blockchain.

There are those who think this ever-increasing blockchain size introduces concerns such as storage capacity, synchronization and even speed of processing transactions.

Hopefully, these issues will be addressed even as Bitcoin users continue to grow in number every day.

Other Applications of the Blockchain

Blockchain technology is attracting many organizations including financial institutions such as the stock exchange. These organizations have seen the potential in the technology, and many have employed software companies to develop a blockchain that is specific to their needs.

Other companies that have seen the potential in blockchain software include elections management organizations, insurance companies, and government departments in charge of gun and automobile registration.

Others include health institutions such as hospitals which need reliable medical and health records systems, organizations that register the ownership of antiquities, artworks, payment systems and many others. Recently, one of the largest financial institutions in the world, Goldman Sachs recently revealed that using a blockchain system, it could save up to $6 billion annually. This is a significant amount that shows just how vital the blockchain system is.

Advantages of using Bitcoin

Networks that use Bitcoin's blockchain and DLT (Distributor Ledger Technology) ensure that internal systems are streamlined. This minimizes errors, helps save time, avoids fraud and reduces delays that occur using traditional reconciliation methods.

When Blockchain system is implemented, far fewer errors are encountered compared to other systems. Maintaining electronic ledgers is far cheaper than alternative types. This helps to reduce the number of employees needed to manage operations.

Any chances of fraud, deceit and other illegal activity are significantly minimized as all entries are visible to the entire network. Almost all human involvement in processing transactions, including international operations such as cross-border trade, is confirmed then recorded on the ledger.

There are some challenges with blockchain that need to be addressed. Fortunately, these challenges pale in comparison to the benefits. These are currently being resolved to ensure a smoother and faster blockchain.

Other Popular, Mainstream Cryptocurrencies

Apart from Bitcoin, there are about six other popular cryptocurrencies. While they are nowhere near as popular, widespread, or influential as Bitcoin, their presence in the world of cryptocurrencies cannot be ignored. These six prominent cryptocurrencies are;

1. LiteCoin
2. Ethereum (ETH)
3. Zcash (ZEC)
4. Ripple (XRP)
5. Dash
6. Monero (XMR)

Of these 6, the two most popular are Ethereum and LiteCoin. LiteCoin was launched in 2011 and was among the first to follow Bitcoin. This virtual currency was created by an MIT graduate named Charlie Lee. It is based on an open source global system of payment and resembles Bitcoin in many ways.

The other significant cryptocurrency is Ethereum. It was only launched in 2015 and uses decentralized software platforms which enable transactions. Ethereum is the platform while the currency is known as ether. In 2014, a pre-sale for ether was launched and it received an overwhelming response.

What are the benefits of investing in Bitcoin?

One of the reasons why investors love Bitcoin is its volatility. When investors put their money in Bitcoin in late 2103, its value was $200. Before the end of that year, that figure rose to $1000. This is a five-fold increase in value in just ten months. Since then, Bitcoin has continued to be very volatile with significant price fluctuations.

- Bitcoin is a portable currency: Most major currencies are not very portable or mobile especially in large amounts. This makes it difficult to move money from one country to another. With Bitcoin, transferring money is simplified because there are no restrictions or government controls.

Good returns on investment: An investor who buys Bitcoin can expect a high return on their investment with time. This is because Bitcoin has attracted a lot of interest across the globe. Investors are seeking to benefit from this popular and versatile cryptocurrency that appears to be very promising. If you invest today, you will very soon come across plenty of other investors willing to buy your Bitcoins at a higher price.

- Bitcoin has seen tremendous growth over the last few years: Bitcoin's value has multiplied over 880,000 times since 2010. If you bought $5 worth of Bitcoins 7 years ago, you'd be worth over $4 million today. In 2017 alone, Bitcoin has gained nearly 400%. In just two years, from July 2015 to July 2017, Bitcoin's value has increased by 645%. The price shot from just above $200 to slightly below $1800.

- Limited supply of Bitcoins: There is a limit to the number of Bitcoins that can come into circulation. However, despite limited supply, demand continues to grow. Hundreds of people buy Bitcoins every day, and the demand can only rise. An increase in demand will result in a higher price so your Bitcoins will be worth a lot more.

- There is no central bank control: Bitcoin does not have an oversight authority such as a reserve bank that supervises its operations. There are no government policies, laws or regulations that directly affect it. This fact alone attracts considerable interest from investors, traders and ordinary people.

Bitcoin processing is superfast: If you buy or sell or transact using Bitcoins, then you will experience the speedy transactions and processing times with no delays. There is a very small fee charged, making transactions affordable.

- Bitcoin has no limits: There are no limits to the number of Bitcoins you can own. You are free to buy or sell as much as you can or even transfer from one country to another.

Chapter 2:

Best Sites to Buy Bitcoins

Bitcoin has been in operation since 2009. However, it only started to attract substantial public attention in 2013. There are plenty of investors who have wisely invested their funds in Bitcoin. Similarly, venture capitalists have shored up finances in this virtual currency, putting in $2.2 million in 2012, $88 million in 2013 and a total of $130 million in 2014.

There is currently plenty of money in Bitcoin and the money keeps increasing. If you are like some of us, then you most likely want a piece of the action. Despite its volatility, Bitcoin continues to enjoy steady growth each year. So, how do you benefit from Bitcoin as an ordinary person?

Where to buy Bitcoins

If you want to buy, sell or invest in Bitcoins, then you should find reputable places where they can be bought. Buying Bitcoins has now become a straightforward task. There are established platforms in the US and around the world where you can safely and securely buy and sell Bitcoins.

Coinbase

If you live in the USA, then one of the best places to buy Bitcoins is Coinbase, whose web address is www.coinbase.com. Coinbase is an online platform where anyone can open an account and purchase Bitcoins. Coinbase charges a small markup of 1% over and above the current market rate as commission.

One benefit of buying Bitcoins at Coinbase is that for every $100 of Bitcoin you buy, you get to receive $10 worth of Bitcoins absolutely free. This is a generous offer that you are unlikely to find anywhere else. To buy bitcoins at Coinbase, follow this link: https://www.coinbase.com/join/526e2512bd43060e28000063.

At Coinbase, you can open an account and then link it to your bank account. This arrangement allows you to use money in your bank account to buy Bitcoins directly. You can set up an auto-purchase system to purchase Bitcoins on a set schedule. For instance, you can set up the system so that you buy $100 worth of Bitcoins each week or every month. The only challenge is that you will not be able to control the price of Bitcoin as it fluctuates often.

Bitstamp

Coinbase is not a Bitcoin exchange. It is merely a platform where individuals and businesses can purchase Bitcoins at a markup. A much better place to buy Bitcoins is the online platform Bitstamp. At Bitstamp, you will be buying Bitcoins directly from sellers. The benefit of buying directly from Bitcoin owners is that the markup charged is much lower, ranging between 0.2% and 0.5%.

Liquidity is much higher at Bitstamp because there are ready sellers and buyers. This is not the case at Coinbase as there are no sellers. Coinbase has to find willing sellers elsewhere. This makes Coinbase a slower and costlier Bitcoin platform.

There are other platforms apart from Bitcoin exchanges where you can buy Bitcoins. One of these is LocalBitcoins, www.localBitcoins.com. This site links potential buyers with sellers. It also provides an escrow system to guarantee transactions. When buying Bitcoins, you should take precautions to protect your Bitcoins.

How to buy Bitcoins

Before you proceed to online platforms such as Coinbase to buy Bitcoins, you need to first understand a couple of things such as; how Bitcoins are purchased, in what format they exist and how they are stored. Plenty of first-time buyers still have a lot questions which they need answered. For instance, can Bitcoins be withdrawn at an ATM? Can I deposit them in my bank account?

Bitcoin only exists in digital form. As a cryptocurrency, Bitcoin is not tangible and cannot be seen, touched or held physically. Bitcoin only exists in cyberspace. When you buy, sell or trade in Bitcoins, you may only do so online. It is after you convert your Bitcoins into fiat currencies such as the dollar that you will receive actual cash.

Sign up for a Bitcoin wallet

The first step you need to take before buying Bitcoins is to have a Bitcoin wallet. There are a couple of reputable online platforms where you can buy a digital wallet. Remember, it is in your Bitcoin wallet that all your Bitcoins are stored. One of the best sites to get a secure digital wallet is http://www.blockchain.info/wallet/#/.

On this website, you are able to directly download Bitcoin wallet onto your device, whether it is a laptop, PC or tablet computer. There are Bitcoin wallets designed specifically for Smartphone users. They are in app form and can be downloaded directly to an Android Smartphone or the iPhone. You will be required to fill an online form before you actually get the wallet. It barely takes a minute and your wallet will thereafter be ready.

A typical Bitcoin wallet looks very similar to your online banking account. The wallet displays detailed information and transactions such as specific dates when you bought Bitcoins and so on. Setting up your Bitcoin wallet and buying Bitcoins are both straightforward processes that anyone can accomplish from the comfort of their home or office computer and any other connected device.

Buy Bitcoins using regular cash

Once your Bitcoin wallet is ready, the next step is to log in to Coinbase.com to buy Bitcoins. If you are buying Bitcoin to invest, then only spend money which you can afford to lose. You can keep buying Bitcoin at regular intervals and build up your investment. If you just need Bitcoins for business or transactions, then you should purchase and spend before the value fluctuates.

Coinbase accepts different forms of payment. As a buyer, if you wish to buy Bitcoins, then you can choose from a number of payment systems. Some of the payment systems you can use include the following;

- Use of credit cards such as Visa
- Use of debit cards such as MasterCard
- Direct bank transfer, ACH
- PayPal online payment system

Having a variety of payment systems is good for customers because they get to choose their preferred option. After selecting a preferred method, you then set it up and proceed to buy Bitcoin. The process is fast, secure and convenient.

Opening an account at Coinbase is a straightforward process. Simply visit the website at the URL www.coinbase.com and click on the open-account tab, then follow the instructions provided and your account will immediately be set up.

Once you open an account at Coinbase, you will need to link it to your Bitcoin wallet and to a payment system. This way, you will be able to use your preferred payment system to deposit money into your account at Coinbase.

As soon as the funds land in your Coinbase account, you can them purchase Bitcoins. The Bitcoins are then transferred to your Bitcoin wallet. They will remain safe in your wallet until you need to transact.

You can have both an account and Bitcoin wallet at Coinbase. While it is not mandatory, it is advisable to do so. Having both an account and wallet on the same platform is convenient. You need to ensure that your Bitcoin wallet is secure. Otherwise it can easily be compromised if it lands in the wrong hands and your Bitcoins stolen. A secure wallet is absolutely essential.

You should ensure that you store your Bitcoin wallet in a secure place away from hackers, scammers and digital thieves. Always ensure that your digital wallet has a multi-signature facility. Also, use a strong password with a mixture of alphanumeric and special characters.

A Bitcoin wallet stores your private keys

Your Bitcoin wallet is where you store your private key. Remember, when you buy Bitcoins, you receive two keys. One of these keys is the public key, and the other is your private key. A public key compares closely to your bank account. It can be shared with the public and allows any person to send you Bitcoins.

On the other hand, your private key is akin to your ATM pin. It should never be shared with anyone. Instead, it should be securely stored in your wallet at all times. It should be secured and kept away from hackers and digital criminals who may want to steal from you. Encrypting the password is highly advisable.

Bitcoin price varies from one country to another. Demand and supply forces are the major factors that determine the value of Bitcoin. Sometimes though, the value may rise or fall depending on policies introduced by a government or announcements by a major corporation.

Locations where you can spend your Bitcoins

There are hundreds of places online where you can spend your Bitcoins. If you want to buy products on the internet such as makeup, sunglasses, fashion apparel and others, you can do so with ease using Bitcoins. There are a lot of enterprises around the world that accept Bitcoins. They include restaurants, café's, airlines, hotels, retail outlets, market places and many others.

There are business owners in countries such as China and Greece who use Bitcoins to transfer their funds overseas. In such countries, governments have put restrictions which hinder cross-border movement of currency. But with Bitcoin, this problem is eliminated. You simply take your money, use it to buy Bitcoins, travel overseas and then reclaim your money in your preferred currency.

The actual Bitcoins that you buy are simply assigned to you and link back to the ledger through a sophisticated encryption algorithm. It is your private key that authorizes transactions and is the one that is stored in your wallet. You can choose to store your wallet offline for the best security. When it is offline, neither the best hacker nor the most harmful malware and viruses can affect it. If you choose to store your wallet online, then ensure its password is encrypted using vital password. At Coinbase, you will be protected by the secure multisig vault.

As Bitcoin grows and becomes hugely popular in America and around the world, you need to know about some factors which may affect its value. These include government taxation policies, the legality of cryptocurrencies and so on. Bitcoin is a valuable currency, but it is still going through nascent stages so caution is advised, especially when trading. Volatility is the most prominent factor that affects Bitcoin value.

Chapter 3:
Where to Store your Bitcoins

Bitcoin wallets

If you intend to buy, invest or deal in Bitcoins, then you should get a Bitcoin wallet. This is a digital wallet that you download to your device and it is where your Bitcoin keys will be stored. Whenever you need to spend or send some funds, you will use the keys to make the payments.

Different types of Bitcoin wallets

There are different types of Bitcoin wallets available. They are designed for different devices and specific needs. For instance, there is a paper wallet available for those who do not want to keep their private keys online. Either way, your wallet should always be backed up. This is to keep your Bitcoin safe because you just never know what could happen and there is no need of taking any risks.

Bitcoins are just like any other type of currency the only difference is that they are not tangible. The use of Bitcoin in business is now widespread. A consumer can use Bitcoins to buy goods, pay for services like booking hotels and even pay for meals in restaurants.

Companies such as Dell, Microsoft, and other corporations also accept Bitcoin payments. You can buy products such as computers, printers, phones and shoes using Bitcoins. To pay using Bitcoins, you will need a secure wallet. Just like cash is stored in wallets, Bitcoins are stored in digital wallets.

Best way to store your Bitcoins

Once you buy some Bitcoins, you will need to store them safely somewhere. One of the best places to do so is in a secure Bitcoin wallet. You can find a reliable Bitcoin wallet at https://www.blockchain.info/wallet/#/.

Another secure digital wallet to consider is the Ledger Nano S Bitcoin wallet. This wallet is one of the top Bitcoin wallets where you can safely and securely store your Bitcoins. Ledger Nano S is the leading hardware wallet and is based on practical, robust and structured safety features.

This wallet can connect to a device such as a computer via USB. It also uses a secure OLED display to confirm every transaction with just a mere tap on the side buttons. You can now get your own offline wallet at www.ledgerwallet.com/r/2d62.

There are different types of digital wallets for storing Bitcoin

1. Mobile wallets

A mobile Bitcoin wallet is designed specifically for your Smartphone. There are portable wallets designed just for the iPhone and others for the Android Smartphone. Think about a person out in the street who enters a store to buy something. Or think about a couple at a restaurant. A mobile Bitcoin wallet will ease payments for customers and enable them to pay for the services they receive and the goods that they need.

Bitcoin wallets can make use of NFC or Near Field Technology which is designed explicitly for mobile phone payments. There are hundreds of millions of Smartphone users out there. A good number of them will find the Bitcoin wallet a useful app to have.

Full Bitcoin clients

Mobile Bitcoin wallets are not full Bitcoin clients. This means that they do not consist of the entire blockchain. It would be too costly and too bulky to download the blockchain onto a mobile device. Most Smartphones cannot hold the blockchain.

A full Bitcoin client is one that downloads and stores the entire blockchain. The Bitcoin blockchain is always growing. Mobile Bitcoin wallets are designated as Simplified Payment Verification (SPV) programs. They only download a minute subset of the entire blockchain. They rely on particular nodes within the blockchain network which ensures that these SPVs have the right and sufficient information at any given time.

Examples of the Bitcoin mobile wallet include Xapo, Mycelium, and the Android-based Bitcoin wallet. However, Apple has not been too keen to approve iPhone Bitcoin wallets. Only recently have these now started becoming popular.

2. Desktop wallets

Another popular wallet is the desktop wallet. Anyone who already has a Bitcoin Core should also have a desktop wallet. Bitcoin Core is powerful software that helps users create a digital wallet which they can use to buy, send or receive Bitcoins. It can also securely store your private key so that it is safe from misuse and wrongful access by cybercriminals.

There are other desktop wallets out there as well. A good example is Multi-Bit. This desktop wallet runs on different operating systems such as Linux, Mac OSX, and Windows. Another desktop wallet that is somewhat popular is Hive. It is an OSX based wallet that comes with exciting and unique features. It includes an app store link that can directly connect to all Bitcoin-based services.

There are Bitcoin desktop wallets that are designed with specific concerns such as security. One such wallet is the Armory. It ensures that any Bitcoin keys stored here cannot be accessed or stolen by anyone. Others are focused more on privacy and anonymity such as the Dark Wallet. This particular wallet is designed for use with a very lightweight browser plug-in when in use. It is intended to also exchange coins so that it becomes difficult to track down users.

3. Hardware wallets

Did you know that there are hardware wallets available? Even though they are limited in number, they are dedicated devices that can store private keys digitally and also facilitate payments. Take, for instance, the Trezor hardware wallet. This particular Bitcoin wallet is meant for investors who wish to purchase substantial amounts of Bitcoin. Most of these large Bitcoin holders usually do not want to entrust their Bitcoins to a third-party.

Yet another hardware Bitcoin wallet is the Ledger US wallet. This is a compact ledger wallet for Bitcoins that uses a smart card for security purposes. It was launched by

Keep-Key as a hardware wallet in September 2015. If you want to secure your Bitcoins, then this particular hardware comes highly recommended.

4. Paper wallets

You can also store your Bitcoins, or the private keys to your Bitcoins on a paper wallet. This is one of the cheapest yet most popular options available to all Bitcoin holders. There are firms that offer the paper wallets. What happens is that when you receive paper wallet, the platform will generate a Bitcoin address for you.

The platform also creates an image that comes with dual QR codes. Of these two codes, one is the public address while the other is the private key. The public address is the one you use to receive Bitcoins while the private one is the one used to shop, pay for goods and transfer money to others.

The benefit of using a paper wallet is that there is no record of your keys anywhere on the Internet. Since there is no record, your Bitcoins will be secure and safe from any form of compromise such as hacking. It is better to be safe than sorry and using a paper wallet is one of the best ways to secure your Bitcoin.

Precaution with Bitcoin wallets

It is crucial to take precaution when handling Bitcoin wallets. You need to manage them with extra care. The private key that you store in the wallet is the key to accessing your Bitcoin. In fact, it is the only way to access your Bitcoins. Should you mess it up by losing, misplacing or in any other way compromise it, then you could very likely lose all your Bitcoins. Therefore, ensure that your wallets remain safe, and neither get lost nor stolen.

Traders and investors need reassurance that Bitcoin is entirely anonymous. By its very nature, Bitcoin is completely anonymous, and users cannot be identified. However, all Bitcoin transactions are visible on the blockchain ledger. This ensures all transactions are trackable and transparent. The term pseudonymous is widely applied to imply precisely this type of Bitcoin transactions.

There are some private companies that have come up with plans to track all Bitcoin transactions and record them on the blockchain. There is also a crowdfunded app under development that helps to improve the privacy of Bitcoin transactions. This app is known as the Dark Wallet and is designed specially for applications that can coin-mix in order to produce stealth wallet addresses.

To secure your Bitcoin wallet, you need to do a couple of things. These include;

- Encrypt the Bitcoin wallet
- Provide a backup
- Get it offline
- Use multisig

Encrypt your Bitcoin wallet

You should ensure that you encrypt your Bitcoin wallet. Do this using a highly secure password. A good password is at least ten characters long that include uppercase, lowercase, numeric and alphanumeric characters. This will ensure that the password is sufficiently complex and no person can access your wallet. Ensure that there is no malware on your computer that could compromise your Bitcoin wallet.

Back it up

Your Bitcoin wallet should be backed up to secure it. Let's say you encrypt your wallet and then store your private key inside. Should you misplace or get it corrupted, then you could lose your wallet and all your Bitcoins too. Backing up the entire Bitcoin wallet at different locations is highly advised.

Use multisig

Multi-sig stands for multiple signatures. There are several devices in the market today that support multisig transactions. Addresses with multi-sig enable users to incorporate a second or even third person to append their signature for an operation to take place. Transactions will only take place once all signatories provide their signatures.

Take the wallet offline

It is advisable to take your Bitcoin wallet offline. There are plenty of Bitcoin owners who are quite jittery about their Bitcoin wallets remaining online. Their fears are not unfounded as the risks of hacking and unauthorized access are real.

The best option is to find a cold storage wallet. There are excellent offline wallets available. These particular Bitcoin wallets will store your private Bitcoin keys offline ensuring that they cannot be stolen, compromised or lost. Most of the regular Bitcoin wallets have on option for offline wallet storage. It is advisable if you hold large amounts of Bitcoins to take your wallet offline just to be safe and avoid unnecessary risks. You can buy an offline wallet here; https://www.ledgerwallet.com/r/2d62.

Chapter 4:
Mining Bitcoin at Home

How Bitcoin comes into existence

Bitcoin is a virtual currency and is neither printed nor minted like normal currencies. Rather, Bitcoins are produced through a process known as mining. Investors are turning to Bitcoin mining as a source of currency. It has numerous benefits over regular currencies. The increased number of Bitcoin users has resulted in its value rising to $4000 mark as of July of 2017.

If you want to benefit from the popularity and rapid increase in the value of Bitcoin, then you should consider becoming a Bitcoin miner. You can begin mining Bitcoin from home using special computers. There are entrepreneurs who are now earning a reliable income simply by mining Bitcoin at home. Bitcoin mining process is well structured and designed using latest software technology so that only a specific number of Bitcoins can be mined.

Bitcoin needs miners

Bitcoin users around the world regularly send the currency to other people such as family and friends. They also spend their Bitcoins across the various outlets that accept it. Some are used to pay for goods and services while others are invested or transferred to different people and for varying reasons.

A miner's job is to generate new Bitcoins and to confirm the accuracy of each transaction. Once confirmed, the transactions are then record on the blockchain.

Miners ensure that all transactions are verified and recorded on the blockchain and are accessible to every member of the network. Anyone connected to the Bitcoin network is then able to view transactions which are frequently updated.

This shows how important Bitcoin miners are. They contribute to the success of Bitcoin system because they verify all transactions and maintain the integrity of the network.

Bitcoin mining at Genesis Mining

Genesis Mining is one of the best online platforms to mine new Bitcoins. Bitcoin miners are required to do only two things;

- They verify Bitcoin transactions
- They mine new Bitcoins

Genesis mining is a cryptocurrency mining company. The company employs experts to ensure the process of Bitcoin mining proceeds smoothly. Most of the experts working for this firm are computer programmers and software engineers.

Who can participate in Bitcoin mining?

Any interested person can join Genesis Mining and start generating new Bitcoins and verifying Bitcoin transactions. If you have some money and are willing to invest, then you may consider joining Genesis Mining program. This particular one offered at Genesis Mining is designed for people who are new to Bitcoin and the world of cryptocurrencies. It is also suitable for large-scale investors.

Genesis Mining is the world's first and best large-scale, multi-algorithm Bitcoin mining service. It operates on a cloud so anyone can join regardless of where they are located. This is an excellent opportunity for investors who would love a chance to invest in Bitcoin and altcoin mining. Altcoin refers to all other cryptocurrencies that compete against Bitcoin.

Genesis Mining offers an excellent opportunity to anyone seeking an opportunity to benefit from cryptocurrency mining. While mining is a productive process to engage in, sufficient skill will be required on your part. Online Bitcoin mining offers a simpler pathway to this process. The process is also known as cloud mining because access is provided via a cloud network. You can also start mining and get a 3% discount if you use the code LPQ5Y. Just follow this link for more information: https://www.genesis-mining.com/.

Is Bitcoin mining a profitable venture?

Bitcoin mining can be a profitable venture but only for those willing to invest sufficiently. It means acquiring the right equipment for the job as well as following the correct procedures. You can use a mining calculator to determine if the Bitcoin mining process will be profitable. Some of the factors that should be considered when using a mining calculator include the following;

- Cost of the hardware used for Bitcoin mining
- Cost of electricity
- Any costs associated with hiring experts such as software programmers

Terms associated with Bitcoin mining

Hash rate: The term hash is a mathematical challenge that a miner's computer has to solve. The hash rate is, therefore, the rate at which the mathematical puzzle is solved. More miners within the Bitcoin network means the hash rate will get higher.

Bitcoins per block: As soon as a hash, or mathematical challenge, is solved, a set number of Bitcoins are created and released. The number of Bitcoins generated started at 50 but is currently at 12.5. Therefore, only 12.5 Bitcoins are created for each hash that is solved.

Bitcoin difficulty: The Bitcoin network was designed to allow only a set number of Bitcoins to be released every 10 minutes. Therefore, the ease or difficulty of solving mathematical bills will depend on the number of miners within the network. It gets harder to solve mathematical puzzles when the hash rate is high. The puzzle is easier to solve when the hash rate is lower.

Pool fees: Bitcoin miners often work in groups to ease the load of solving mathematical puzzles. A group of miners can also be referred to as a pool because they pool together minds, resources and so on.

A mining pool, therefore, consists of a group of miners who come together to make Bitcoin mining more efficient. Members of the pool contribute some money to a kitty to meet their operation and running costs and any overheads. The fee per miner is referred to as the pool fee.

Power consumption: The process of Bitcoin mining consumes a lot of energy. Power consumed by the computers used should be determined because it affects profitability. Therefore, every Bitcoin mining pool should find out the power consumed to solve a single mathematical puzzle, so they understand the rate of power consumption.

Conversion rate: One of the challenges of Bitcoin mining is that the rate of conversion of new Bitcoins to dollars is not known. Whether Bitcoin is profitable to mine or not is unknown because of this. This should be a concern if you plan to mine and hold onto your Bitcoins.

Bitcoin mining calculator

If you decide that you want to become a Bitcoin miner, then you will need a mining calculator. This is a powerful software program that helps you determine whether your Bitcoin mining process will be successful or not. The calculator takes into consideration all the different aspects associated with Bitcoin mining.

What you need for successful Bitcoin mining

The first thing you will need to start Bitcoin mining is a Bitcoin wallet. Each Bitcoin wallet carries its unique address. A digital wallet such as the Bitcoin wallet is essentially an encrypted online bank account which safely holds all that you earn as you mine Bitcoins. Also essential are the tools needed for the mining process. Having all the right equipment and tools is essential. Here is a look at some of these machines;

GPU/CPU for Bitcoin mining: In the early days of Bitcoin mining, miners often used CPUs to effect the mining process. Ordinary desktop computers were capable of handling the mining process. Today, you will need a more powerful GPU mining computer using GPU graphics cards.

GPUs used today are almost 100 times faster and more powerful than CPUs used back then. The more powerful and faster a computer is, the more successful the miners will be.

FPGA Bitcoin mining: It is now possible for manufacturers of Bitcoin mining equipment to purchase and customize kits using a FPGA or field-programmable gate array. Using this gate array, computer chips can be bought in bulk and then tailored for the specific purpose of Bitcoin mining.

ASIC Bitcoin mining: ASIC stands for application-specific integrated circuits. These are the latest and most efficient Bitcoin processing machines currently in use. These computer chips are designed for delivering mining power at super high speeds. However, the ASICS chips were designed for specific tasks and use very little electricity. They are also very expensive to produce.

Why should you mine Bitcoins?

Successful and unique solution

If you choose to mine Bitcoins through a reputable and established firm such as Genesis Mining, then you will be part of their efficient and unique solution which has been used successfully over the years.

A lot of Bitcoin mining processes currently underway take place in overcrowded Bitcoin farm markets. Direct mining of Bitcoins using powerful, dedicated GPUs with programmable chips ensures a smooth operation where all participants benefit.

Profitable cryptocurrency mining process

Any investor who invests significantly in a process such as Bitcoin mining does so with the hope that not only will they recoup their investment but also earn a decent income for a long time. This is possible with Genesis Mining. As a leading Bitcoin mining firm, Genesis can generate Bitcoins fast enough so that all pool members benefit financially and share in the profits earned.

Positive experience mining Bitcoins

You get to sign up with a reputable company whose systems and structures work efficiently. Initially, Bitcoin mining was a stressful process with computers breaking down, high power bills and so on. All these challenges have since been addressed.

Mining Bitcoins and altcoins simultaneously

It is important to note that Bitcoins and altcoins can be mined all at the same time using the latest hardware and software. If for instance, you are interested in mining Bitcoins, then you can do so exclusively. However, if you wish to engage in the mining of other altcoins such as LiteCoin and Ethereum, then this is also possible.

ETHEREUM

Bitcoin continues to be a favorite digital currency that is in high demand and accepted round the world. It remains a decentralized currency that is produced through a community and not overseen by any central authority, any central bank or even governments.

Anyone is free to join this community and buy, use and deal in Bitcoins. It is almost free to transfer Bitcoins from one person to another and from one account to another. You can trade, sell, buy things and receive Bitcoins as a trader. This is how flexible Bitcoin is. However, there are limits as to how many Bitcoins can be produced.

Bitcoin is produced digitally and held online. It is unlike other currencies such as the dollar, Euro, yen, pound and so on. Bitcoins are mined or produced using a network of connected computers that rely on unique software and hardware. There are many reasons why people love Bitcoin and why they will continue to use it even in the years to come.

By joining a trusted site such as Genesis Mining, you will be partnering with a professional team of experts who will guide you and ensure you share in the profits generated. There are a lot of successful investors that have joined Genesis Mining. You will receive bonuses and discounts upon joining. You can find out more about Bitcoin mining with Genesis at www.genesis-mining.com.

Chapter 5:

Investing in Bitcoin

Growth and investment in Bitcoin

Over the last couple of years, Bitcoin has received a lot of funds from venture capitalists. These are reliable investors who have assessed Bitcoin network fundamentals, prospects, and current performance and determined that an investment in Bitcoin is a worthy venture.

In 2012, investors and venture capital firms invested only $2.2 million into Bitcoins. In just the first six months of 2014, they put in a total of $130 million. In 2013, the total amount invested amounted to $88 million. These figures are a clear indication of the popularity of Bitcoin and the kind of confidence that investors have in it.

Bitcoin investing for the average person

For individual investors, one of the best ways of investing in Bitcoin is to buy and hold. This is the traditional way of investing. However, due to the volatile nature of Bitcoin, it is prudent for an investor to only invest money which they can afford to lose. If not, then the fluctuation in prices could severely dent your savings.

Buying Bitcoins online is a straightforward process. All you need to do is to get onto your preferred site such as BitConnect, open an account, link it with a payment system such as a credit card and then click the buy button. Now all you need is a wallet to store the Bitcoins that you buy.

It is also advisable to buy and hold, so you benefit in the long term. Many investors, especially smallholders, often rush to dispose of their Bitcoins as soon as the price goes up. While this makes immediate sense, it is not a good long-term strategy. It also causes Bitcoin to remain very volatile. To reduce the volatility and keep Bitcoin stable, investors should buy then hold onto their Bitcoins.

While it is almost free to transact using Bitcoins, the exchanges often charge a small overhead. This amount is about 1% of the transaction cost. Take for instance Coinbase. This is not a Bitcoin exchange, so they charge a fee of 1% per transaction, whether you wish to purchase or trade in Bitcoins.

Make money online with BitConnect

There is a considerable number of investors around the world who are searching for ways to invest in Bitcoins. Others are looking to access, trade and use Bitcoin for commerce. They want reassurance that using Bitcoin is safe and worthwhile.

Bitconnect

Bitconnect is a community of like-minded individuals operating on an open source platform. It has garnered a reputation of building trust and security in the Bitcoin and cryptocurrency communities.

The Bitconnect platform connects members both financially and socially so they achieve their goals of security and financial independence. All these opportunities have been lacking for a long time.

Bitconnect Investment Program

Investing in Bitcoins is risky mainly due to its volatility. But with the trusted Bitconnect Lending, the risk is eliminated. This is a trusted system that allows members to pool their resources and share in the profits as they gain interest.

Bitconnect, unlike the others, uses state-of-the-art volatility software to generate significant gains for its members. This software is known as the Bitconnect Trading Bot. These profits are shared equitably among all the members. For more information, click on this link: https://bitconnect.co/?ref=cryptofuture.

Bitconnect Trading Bot

If you become a member of Bitconnect, then you stand to earn up to 40% in interest if you invest in one of the four levels of investing on offer. These levels are Tier 1, Tier 2, Tier 3, and Tier 4.

Bitconnect investment levels

At Tier 1 level, investment amounts range from $100 to $1000. The money is locked in for 299 days and earns an interest during this time.

At Tier 2 level, investment amounts range from $1,010 to $5,000. The capital invested and return on investment is paid out after 239 days. Investors also earn a daily interest of o.1% of their investment each day.

At Tier 3 level, the investment amount now ranges from $5,010 to $10,000. The capital plus a return on investment will be paid out after 179 days. The investor earns 0.2% of their investment each day for the entire investment period.

Tier 4 offers the highest return. Members who opt for this investment level invest between $10,010 and $100,000 for 120 days only. After expiry of the 120 days, the investor receives their capital back including the return on investment. Members also earn 0.25% of the invested amount each day.

Reasons to join Bitconnect

Bitconnect is more than just an investment website. It contains the most up-to-date crypto news. The platform also provides Bitcoin wallet services. This website is an important platform that enables members to achieve their dreams of economic security and financial independence.

Buying Bitcoin

For Americans, Coinbase is one of the best platforms to buy Bitcoins. All you need to do is to get online, open an account and then get a Bitcoin wallet as well. While it is a good idea to get an account and a wallet all from the same platform, it is not mandatory. You can open an account at one Bitcoin platform and then open a Bitcoin wallet elsewhere.

Now, once you have your account open and your Bitcoin wallet connected, you will connect the account to a funding platform. It could be your bank account, a debit or credit account or even an online payment processing platform such as PayPal. This way, you can transfer cash to your Bitcoin account, buy Bitcoins at Coinbase, and then store the Bitcoins in your Bitcoin wallet.

You can also set up an automatic Bitcoin purchase order. This means placing an electronic order on the platform so that Bitcoins are purchased on a regular basis as initially ordered. It could be every week, once every two weeks or even once every month.

Coinbase will buy the Bitcoins for you but remember they are not an exchange. This means they will have to source the Bitcoins from elsewhere. This may institute some delays which can affect the prices.

Bitstamp

You can also purchase Bitcoins at a much better rate and with faster processing times at Bitstamp. Bitstamp is the traditional Bitcoin exchange where buyers and sellers congregate to buy and sell Bitcoins. Therefore, it is more convenient to purchase Bitcoins at this exchange and in sufficient quantities compared to other platforms such as Coinbase.

Bitstamp

Bitstamp charges a small fee of between 0.5% and 0.2% depending on the size of the transaction. If you want faster trades with lower costs, then you should consider buying Bitcoins on platforms such as Bitstamp. You will interact with many buyers and sellers who wish to offer you Bitcoins at different rates. At Bitstamp you can also checkout the profile of a seller so that you deal with an experienced and trustworthy trader.

You should vet any trader before you engage with them. Vetting sellers are not uncommon just because you need to know whom you are dealing with. If a seller has an excellent reputation on their profile with recommendations from other buyers, then you may take a chance to deal with them.

What you may want to avoid is anyone who is offering Bitcoins at very low prices, yet they have a new account with no reviews. Alternatively, you can buy very small amounts of Bitcoins from such a trader just to note whether they are genuine so that you minimize your risks if they turn out to be a fraud.

Good reasons for investing in Bitcoin

According to research, some of the wealthiest individuals in America including some of the most successful entrepreneurs have invested in Bitcoin. They include the richest person in Asia, Mr. Li Ka-Shing, British billionaire Richard Branson, and the owners or founders of eBay, PayPal, and Yahoo.

With such successful people on board, Bitcoin is seen as a solid investment commodity that has been approved by finance experts. It means that investing in this cryptocurrency that has taken the world by storm is a wise move. A lot of investors would be willing to invest in Bitcoin just because of the mark of confidence shown by these successful billionaires.

Several factors make Bitcoin attractive. It overcomes some of the challenges encountered by traditional currencies such as the kroner, the pound, yen, dollar and all the others. Major world currencies face numerous challenges and limitations that Bitcoin is not exposed to.

Benefits of investing in Bitcoin

1. Inflation risks are lower

When compared to other currencies like the dollar, pound or yen, Bitcoin faces a much lower risk due to inflation. This is because it is not controlled by any central authority.

All other currencies are owned, controlled and overseen by their respective governments. It is this reason that sometimes leads to inflation. Governments tax some items more and some policies affect commodities in the markets. These all affect inflation. Fortunately, Bitcoin is not affected by any of these challenges.

Sometimes currencies lose their value, which causes people to part with more money for the same products or services. This, however, does not apply to Bitcoin. The system that Bitcoin uses is infinite which eliminates any possibility of inflation challenges.

2. Bitcoin is not controlled by any government

It is true that there is no government or central authority that controls or manages Bitcoin. No central bank issues policies, whether fiscal or monetary, regarding Bitcoin. This factor alone makes Bitcoin a much stronger currency compared to traditional fiat currencies.

Bitcoin is a global currency that is used, traded and accepted in diverse places all over the world. Since it is not under the control of any government, the chances that it will fail, cause hyperinflation, and things of that nature are close to zero. Therefore, it has a much lower chance of falling compared to all others.

3. Bitcoin transactions are cheap, fast and simple

Compared with other currencies and payment systems, Bitcoin is a very fair system. When you send money from one person to another, the transaction is almost instant, even international transfers. Some other platforms such as banks take up to 3 days to effect payments. These long delays may harm businesses and even individuals.

Many other platforms such as PayPal or credit cards charge significant fees. With Bitcoin, there are almost no fees charged, and all transactions are virtually free. This is true, especially where Bitcoins are exchanged between two individuals or between an individual and a business.

4. Bitcoin is a very portable currency

Compared with other types of currencies, Bitcoin can be said to be the most portable. You can move Bitcoins from countries such as Japan, Australia, and China to the US, UK, and Canada with ease. Bitcoin portability is especially important where large sums of money need to be moved. Government regulations often limit amounts that can leave the country. Bitcoin eliminates this problem because it can be bought in one country and then used in another country.

5. Transactions are anonymous

When you transact using Bitcoins, all your transactions remain anonymous and cannot be tracked. A lot of people around the world value their privacy. People love doing things privately. Sadly, credit cards, banks, and online payment platforms often require a lot of personal information. The information they collect from users is sometimes compromised and even stolen by criminals. If you want to transact privately, then Bitcoin offers you the flexibility and privacy of doing so without breaking any laws.

6. Bitcoin has a bright future

You also need to know that Bitcoin has an incredibly bright future. Everything points to a prosperous future, and that is why people are putting their money in Bitcoin. The returns that people are getting from this global cryptocurrency and the possibilities for the future are almost endless. Those who bought Bitcoins just a few years back are millionaires today. You can be a millionaire in the future if you make the right choices and decisions today.

Chapter 6:

What Is ICO?

Initial Coin Offering

The term ICO stands for Initial Coin Offering. ICO refers to the unregulated means through which cryptocurrencies raise funds for their ventures. A startup such as Bitcoin or Ethereum can issue or announce an ICO to bypass and avoid the highly regulated and rigorous processes related to funding as required by banks and even venture capitalists.

During an ICO process, a significant amount of the cryptocurrencies is made available to initial backers of the project. These backers then provide the financing needed to market, improve or develop further the cryptocurrency. The funding is often in the form of hard currency and at other times in the way of Bitcoins.

The process of issuing an ICO

There is a process that cryptocurrency companies follow when issuing an ICO. The first step is to write a white paper that states the objectives of the issuing firm, the needs of society that the project intends to fulfill, amount of money needed for the project and even the type of money that is required.

Sometimes an ICO involves the sale of a new digital currency at a discounted price or even as a token. The sale is undertaken to raise capital. The first ICO was able to raise over $1 billion. Should the cryptocurrency get the approval of consumers and succeed in the market, then the investors will make money if they sell or retain their cryptocurrencies.

There is a difference between investing in an ICO and an IPO at the stock market. An IPO grants ownership rights to shares of a company while cryptocurrencies in an ICO do not. There is also no ownership provision for investors in the company's stock. Investing in digital or virtual currencies can be a risky affair. It is much riskier than investing in stocks and shares. The motivation of investing in ICOs is governed by the successful and explosive growth in value of currencies such as Bitcoins. A single Bitcoin is now worth just under $4000. This is why there are professional and fanatic investors in most ICOs.

Early ICO investors

Most early investors into cryptocurrencies hope that the virtual money and its technology and system will be successful just the way Bitcoin is. It is evident to any interested person of the phenomenal growth, high interest, and global outlook that Bitcoin currently enjoys.

These investors also hope that they will buy new cryptocurrencies at low, affordable and subsidized prices. Once the new crypto-cash is made available to the public, then the value is expected to go up, and investors hope to recoup some of their money and even make a handsome profit selling the currency.

Successful Ethereum ICO

The most recent ICO announced was for Ethereum. Ethereum has its currency as ethers which can be used online as digital money. This project was successful and plenty of early investors who garnered some smart contracts. This project was announced in 2014 and it went on to raise $18 million.

There are a lot of similarities between an IPO, ICO, and crowd-funding. In all these three funding options money is usually raised from willing participants who are not guaranteed a chance to recoup their finances in any way. Sometimes during an ICO, if the funds raised fail to meet the set amount, then the cash will be returned to its owners.

Is an ICO a big deal?

In 2017 alone, there have been 140 ICOs. These ICOs have in total raised more than $2 billion in token sales. Before then, some experts were of the opinion that ICOs were not a useful source of funding and that they would soon disappear.

After an announcement of an ICO, there is usually a pre-sale. At this stage, buyers contact sellers to initiate a transaction. Sometimes sales are commenced on digital platforms with identity recognition software. ICOs have hugely taken over Silicon Valley. There is a firm belief that there will be new ICOs this year that is expected to raise more than $4 billion. This is a lot of money that will go to Silicon Valley to help improve technology and support the work of developing cryptocurrencies.

ICO and Blockchain technology

According to insiders, for a large number of ICOs issued, only a small amount will successfully raise funds to the tune of millions of dollars. The successful ones are usually the ones that feature blockchain technology. It is a compelling technology and beneficial in many ways.

The reason why blockchain is trusted is that of its technology. Blockchain features a transparent network that makes it easy and open for users to note all transactions within the system. And to cap it all, there has been a success in the use of blockchain, especially with Bitcoin which uses this technology exclusively.

Most early investors into cryptocurrencies peg their hopes that the virtual money and its technology and system will be successful just the way Bitcoin is.

It is evident to all people of the phenomenal growth, high interest, and global outlook that Bitcoin now enjoys. Bitcoin is currently the largest and by far the most successful network in the entire world. Bitcoin is successful primarily due to its anonymous nature as well as an open and accountable system.

Successful ICOs

Although there are many successful ICOs, there are others that have not been so successful. Investors are cautioned to select their ICOs very careful because not all projects funded by ICOs are poised to succeed. Some may not turn out as well as hoped, so it is good to undertake due diligence before investing.

Again, some of these operations are not overseen by government authorities such as the SEC, the Securities and Exchange Commission so it is possible to lose funds. Still, great caution is necessary on the part of investors. However, most companies putting out an ICO are well known in Silicon Valley, some have been around for years, and there is proof of concept and signs of successful ventures.

ICOs are similar, yet different to IPOs. The former usually deals with supporters and venture capitalists while the latter is associated with investors. In crowd funding projects, backers often support a cause and hardly need their money back because they are mostly donors. This is why ICOs are also referred to by others as crowdsafe.

Investing in an ICO through Bankera

There are many good reasons for investing in a good ICO. Most of the companies issuing ICOs are in the tech sector and specifically in cryptocurrencies. They have proven to be very successful in the last couple of years. Top among these is Bitcoin followed by LiteCoin at a distant second then the others like Ethereum.

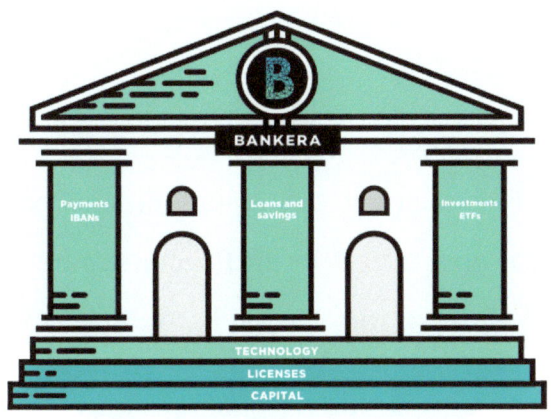

Now, Bankera has announced a pre-ICO. This ICO is for a revolutionary blockchain bank. There are excellent prospects here because this will be among the first online financial institutions that operate exclusively on cryptocurrencies.

Bankera is a digital FinTech solution platform. The firm is hoping to interrupt the banking and financial services world by introducing very innovative banking solutions. These banking solutions aim to reduce the costs of banking to customers and make transactions faster and more transparent.

The firm is currently fundraising and preparing for the ICO or Initial Coin Offer. You can now participate in this offer and enjoy high returns within a short period. Members of the public are welcome to join in this ICO. You can participate through this link: https://www.bankera.com/?ref=3700170522. When you click on this link, you will be able to join and participate together with other investors and become part of an elite group who will revolutionize the banking sector.

As it is, I have invested my money into this ICO. I have also invited my family and close friends to invest and share in this upcoming venture. If you want to enjoy huge profits benefits, then this new online banking venture is where you should put your money.

More information about Bankera

Bankera launched in 2017 and is a subsidiary of the successful and popular and successful firm SpectroCoin. SpectroCoin is a cryptocurrency exchange, a payment processor and also an e-wallet and debit card provider.

Bankera is hoping to interrupt the banking and financial services world by introducing very innovative banking solutions. The purpose of this bank is to provide solutions that will reduce the costs of banking to customers and make transactions faster and more transparent.

Some of the services that Bankera is expected to provide include provision of debit cards, payment processing solutions and customer payment accounts that feature IBAN foreign exchange rates. These services will support both fiat currencies such as the dollar as well as cryptocurrencies such as Bitcoin.

The firm already has the necessary IT arrangements as well as regulatory authority. They have put together a board that will oversee the operations of the bank. Some of the members of the board include renowned experts in the field of finance such as Antanas Guoga who is a member of the

European Parliament and Lon Wong who is the president of NEM.io foundation.

Conclusion

Thank you for making it through to the end of this book. Let's hope it has been informative and has provided you with all the tools you need to achieve your goals whatever they may be.

The next step is to follow the guidelines provided in the book and then find out where you best fit within the Bitcoin structure. Currently, anyone investing in Bitcoins and other cryptocurrencies stands to make significant profits in the coming days. This is because there is a lot of interest in cryptocurrencies, especially Bitcoin. Many individual investors and also institutional investors have invested their resources in Bitcoin and other cryptocurrencies over the last few years. The returns have been very encouraging.

The value of Bitcoin has gone up almost 10-fold in the last two years. The price has already crossed the $5000 mark as of October 2017. Bitcoin is largely used in America even though interest is growing in Europe and Asia. This just goes to show the kind of success it is enjoying in the market. Experts contend this trend will only keep growing for years to come. There are many different ways of investing in cryptocurrencies. One of these is to invest in an ICO. This is an Initial Coin Offer where a cryptocurrency firm offers its currency to willing investors and buyers at a discounted rate.

Alternatively, you can invest in Bitcoin by purchasing it at specific platforms. Take for instance Bitconnect. This is a renowned Bitcoin firm where you invest in Bitcoins and then receive daily payouts depending on the choice of package. You can also choose to join a Bitcoin mining operation. Many people are doing this through trusted platforms such as Genesis Mining. If you do this, then you will successfully confirm Bitcoin transactions in the blockchain network. You will also mine new Bitcoins which will then be put into circulation.

Description

Do you enjoy confirming transactions and generating new money? Do you love sitting back and watching your money grow? Then you should invest and trade in cryptocurrencies. This book has been written to inform and advise you about investing in cryptocurrencies like Bitcoin.

By reading this book, you will acquire useful information that you need to be successful with in cryptocurrency venture.

Some of the things you will learn include;

- Basic information about Bitcoin
- How and where to buy Bitcoins
- Where to store your Bitcoin
- How to successfully invest in Bitcoins
- And so much more!

A lot of traders and investors have been investing their money in Bitcoin and using it for trade and as an investment tool. The kind of gains that Bitcoin has seen over the last few years and the growing interest from traders around the world can only mean that the prospects are very lucrative.

www.ingramcontent.com/pod-product-compliance
Lightning Source LLC
Chambersburg PA
CBHW040225220526
45473CB00001B/123